José Martínez Juárez

Event Design

How to create a business plan for congresses, conventions, trade shows and corporate events

Event Design: How to create a business plan for congresses, conventions, trade shows and corporate events.

First edition: July 2020

Copyright 2019, José Martínez Juárez

www.josemartinezjuarez.com

INDAUTOR, Registration Number 03-2019-121109411200-01

ISBN: 97-986-639928-48

Cover photo: Chuttersnap- Unsplash

Acknowledgment

This book is a tribute to all those friends, teachers, and colleagues who have been part of my professional career within the event industry.

I especially want to thank my three mentors: Elena Maribona founder of Expo Pack México, Less Weir from Reed Exhibitions and Chuck Yuska from PMMI for sharing with me their knowledge, experience and above all for their trust expressed on all those occasions we have had the opportunity to collaborate together, to you my most sincere appreciation.

I want to particularly mention Rosa Monzó, director of the ESDAI Postgraduate and External Training and Consulting department from the Universidad Panamericana in Mexico City, who opened me the doors to the world of teaching, an activity that inspired me to create this book for all those students and professionals who are looking to get a deeper knowledge of the fascinating world of EVENT DESIGN.

All my love to Gaby, Pao and Abraham for always giving me their unconditional support.

Index

Introduction

Humans are essentially social beings, the interaction with one another is the motive that brace our existence and personal development, for this reason, even with all the technology that today communicates and unites us, the event business will continue to grow and professionalize.

This book is a tool that will allow you, the organizer, operator, agency, or event professional, to develop new events and visualize the potential for their realization.

By following the different topics covered in this book, you will be able to realize if your event is feasible and you will have the certainty of having considered aspects that perhaps you had not taken before into consideration.

This methodology has been especially useful to me in more than twenty-five years of professional activity, in which I have faced the creation and administration of various events. It is also one of the subjects that I teach in various educational institutions and a recurring topic in the talks and seminars that I share in different forums.

Event Types

There are a variety of ways to classify events, I particularly like to use a quite simple and direct classification:

Events according to their nature:

- Social Events

- Corporate or Business Events

- Cultural Events

- Religious Events

- Scientific and Academic Events

- Political Events

- Sport Events

This book is specifically designed to help you develop corporate or business events, although it also covers topics that are useful for any other type of event.

Corporate events

- *Congress* - Essentially an academic event where various topics of common interest are discussed. The invitation is open to the public and each participant pays for their registration.

- *Convention* - Event where commercial topics related to a market, brand or product are discussed; its call is by invitation and generally limited to a select audience. The participant generally attends on behalf of his company, who in turn pays his registration.

- *Trade show* – Event produced to launch, promote, and market products and services of an industry or sector to a target audience or to the general public. (in Spain and Latin America, the term "Feria" is used; in México the term "Exposición" is used)

- *Fairs* - Popular celebration that includes gastronomic, commercial and entertainment areas.

- *Press conference* - Event where the press and media are gathered to receive relevant information about a brand, product, or service, and is invited to advertise through its different channels.

- *Inauguration* - Official opening ceremony of an event.

- *Product presentation* - Activations and events designed to launch a product or service to a target market and to the press and media.

- *Summit* - Event where the participants are the highest levels of a group or company.

- *Panels* - Expert discussion and exchange of ideas, where they review and discuss a central theme.

- *Cycle of Conferences* - Event designed to promote discussion, research, and dissemination of one or more topics, in which various specialists or academics participate as speakers; it usually ends with a question and answer session.

- *Corporate Events* - They are held by a company for various reasons, among which are: generating stimuli to productivity, causing coexistence and integration among colleagues ("team building"), anniversaries or celebrations, as well as for internal decision-making in a company.

- *Online Events* - Events run through a digital platform, that allow the interaction of the attendees sharing their materials, opinions, and screens digitally; they increase the interaction of diverse geographic groups by not requiring the transportation of attendees and are an economic alternative due to the fact that other traditional hospitality services such as lodging and food are not required.

- *Virtual Events* - Events run through a virtual reality environment; the participants see and hear a real-life interactive experience using avatars and attending virtual venues, conference rooms and environments.

Business Operation Plan (BOP)

"Inspiration exists, but it has to find you working"
PABLO PICASSO

The Business Operation Plan is a tool that facilitates the viability analysis of a business project, with the understanding that a business is an activity that seeks to obtain a profit, that is: "a profitable event" (preferably with possibility for repetition to create a virtuous cycle of income). It is also an analysis of the "why" and the "for what" of my event and how will I benefit others and how to obtain a financial benefit.

You should start by developing a detailed and organized description of all conceptual and operational elements, in addition to establishing general objectives and financial objectives by identifying the resources necessary to produce the event.

An event requires the following types of resources: material, human, technological, and financial. By clearly defining these resources, we have a more concrete idea of everything we need to organize.

Many of the events currently taking place are non-profit; however, the mere realization of the event implies the use and administration of resources, therefore, having a BOP where these resources are defined and quantified, ensures a well-achieved event.

The idea of this tool is to have enough information to achieve a more solid event, there are times when at the end of our BOP we discover that the event we have planned lacks some key element such as a large enough market or that there are very few companies interested in the segment or topic. It may be that due to the nature of a market, companies or visitors have little chance of participating; therefore, the project is a nominee to be reevaluated or even canceled.

Developing a BOP goes beyond being crammed with data and figures, it is a tool that allows us to have a clear idea of our project, as well as helping us to have greater certainty that it will be profitable.

Ideally at the end of our journey, we will have a clear idea of:

- A detailed description of the event
- Reasons that justify the event proposal
  Why is it necessary to do this event?
- Goals to be achieved
- Differentiating characteristics against similar events
- Competitive advantages
- Investment required
- Expected profitability
- Certainty for the fulfillment of the event

Briefing

The "Briefing" is a condensed description of our event.

Is the culmination of the time invested during the design of our BOP and therefore it is written and defined at the end, when we have already compiled all the information and have follow through a detailed analysis.

In the "Briefing", we must accurately summarize the following:

- Event name
- Event dates
- Host city and venue
- Type of event: congress, convention, trade show, etc.
- Edition number
- Objective
- Number of Attendees
- Total surface and areas
- Types of products showcased
- Visitor profile
- Food & Beverages if required
- Conference or marketing activation program
- Promotion and advertising plan
- Contact information
- Web page

This condensed information is very useful, it helps us to have in a concise text the entire description of the event, we can even use it as the presentation piece for potential clients, sponsors and visitors, it is also a fundamental part of the sales material.

Always remember that the Briefing is written and defined once we have already completed our BOP.

BRIEFING EXAMPLE

ART CRAFTS FESTIVAL

"HANDS OF THE WORLD"

DATES: October 10-13, 2025
TIMINGS: 11:30 a.m. to 8:00 p.m.
VENUE: Sacramento Convention Center, CA
EDITION: First
TYPE: B2B commercial festival (Business to Business) and B2C (Business to Consumer)

PURPOSE OF THE EVENT: Promote art crafts from different parts of the world and encourage their use as part of decoration trends and in daily life.

ESTIMATED ASSISTANCE: 1,000 professional buyers and 5,000 general attendees.

SURFACE OF THE EVENT: 65,000 square feet. Commercial area, gastronomic area, and activation area.

EXHIBITORS: Manufacturers, importers, and distributors of national and international handicrafts.

- Textiles.

- Glass crafts.
- Leather goods.
- Metal crafts.
- Clay crafts.
- Furniture and accessories.
- Jewelry.
- Ceramics.
- Marble and stone.
- Vegetable fiber crafts.
- Various.

VISITOR PROFILE:

Professional: Interior designers, decorators, architects, designers and owners of gift and decoration stores.

General public: women and men, NSE A / B, C +, ages 21 and up interested in culture, design, architecture, and interior design.

ACTIVATIONS:
Ceramic workshop - Embassy of Italy
Leather Goods Workshop - Texas State Government
Clay workshop - Metepec, Mexico

PROMOTION AND ADVERTISING: Electronic newsletter that will be promoted among interior designers, industrial designers, and architects.
    -360 media campaign: electronic, specialized media, press, radio, TV, and PR.
-    Internet page with a blog specialized in art crafts and interior design.

CONTACT INFORMATION:
Successful Events
         contact @ handsoftheworld.com
         Mobile 4469 1106
         Office 5081 1109

Web page: handsoftheworld.com

Market Research

"Amazing things happen when you listen to the customer"
JONATHAN MIDENHALL

A market research is the analysis we make of the industry or sector to which the event is aimed, it includes the trends that are affecting this market, it helps us understand the competitors and get to know the attendees to detail.

Industry or economic sector size.

When we decide to design an event, knowing the size of the industry or sector to which it is directed, gives us a precise idea of its strength, as well as the accomplishment potential; It also helps us understand if it can be held not only once but several times and therefore ensure its repetition and increase its profitability in the future.

Strong or distinctive industries or sectors exist in all countries; for example, in Mexico the automotive manufacturing industry is an interesting niche for professional events and the pharmaceutical and health industry for congresses and conventions, in Colombia the topics related to the textile industry and the production of food and beverages; Chile has great potential for events related to the mining industry, as well as agricultural, wine and fishing events.

The U.S. is especially attractive for holding teambuilding and corporate events, there is a wide variety of thematic venues that allow organizers to develop attractive proposals in addition to a wide variety of destinations with unique characteristics: beaches, modern cities, national & thematic parks, museums and famous restaurants.

Participation in Gross Domestic Product (GDP)

All economic activity is part of the GDP of a country, we can define GDP as the monetary value of goods and services produced by an economy in a given period of time; the importance of a particular industry or sector within the GDP of our country, allows us to measure its strength and potential for events.

The GDP figures are easily traceable from various sources, mainly on the Internet; leaning on them and getting to know them in as much detail as possible, gives us credibility with all the players in that industry who will feel confident when dealing with a professional event organizer .

Growth projection

The events industry is so varied and unique that it can cover practically any economic sector. We can affirm that there is the possibility of holding events on any topic; This is how knowledge and research of the potential of the sector in which we want to develop events becomes a guide to specialize and even project the size and type of events that can be held in the future.

For example, the Mexican toy industry has suffered the arrival of a large number of low-cost toys from Asia; This affects the industry, reducing its growth possibilities and causing a loss of value as a possible niche for holding events; On the other hand, industries such as medical or insurance, are traditionally large consumers of events such as conferences, conventions and incentive trips.

Foreign Sector

It refers to the participation of a given industry in the country's imports and exports; For example, if we develop an event related to video games or apps design in the U.S., we can visualize an important potential to make it international, since that particular sector has strong exports, as well as international players of great weight worldwide, the same case it would be for a coffee event in Colombia.

To explore these data, we can approach the international organizations in charge of promoting exports in each country, such as: Business France-France, ICEX Spain, JETRO-Japan, etc.

When organizing trade shows, this is especially useful, since through the knowledge of the products that are imported into our country, we can strengthen the offer on the show floor, incorporate the participation of country pavilions, or negotiate the support of these organizations related to foreign trade to bring exhibitors of these product categories.

There are also several private companies, especially in Europe and Asia, whose function is to support national manufacturers in the search for markets abroad. These are also companies with which we can sign agreements to promote our event among their clients regionally. They generally function as sales agents, under a commission.

Finally, we can also use the embassies and commercial offices of our country to support us in the promotion of our event in the respective representations they have abroad.

Benchmarking

Is the analysis of capabilities, resources, strategies, competitive advantages, strengths, weaknesses, dates, and other characteristics of current and potential competitor events, both national and international.

This analysis helps us make decisions or formulate strategies that allow us to compete with them in the best possible way; Especially in the event industry, dates play a key role for success.

If we decide to hold a congress on the same dates that the most important company convention in the sector is held, surely its executives and employees will be unable to participate in our congress.

That is why it is essential to make a written list that concentrates all the events that are related to our industry, including their dates and venues, to ensure that the date that we have chosen for our event is the ideal one for that particular industry.

The analysis of competitor events not only allows us to be aware of the new actions or strategies of our competitors, but also to explore the possibility of making alliances, for example if our idea is to launch a gastronomic congress, and there is already an organizer in France with a similar event, there is a possibility of partnering to launch either a local version of the event in your country, or to launch a new event concept that centralizes the strengths that each of the organizers can bring to the project.

Finally, when analyzing our competitors we could discover opportunity niches, for example: one of the weaknesses of an event could be its inability to attract the most important speakers in the industry, as a consequence, we can make the decision to strengthen our program conferences with speakers of greater prestige in order to win the market.

Purchase process and seasonality

Each industry or sector has a purchasing cycle that is governed by consumption patterns; These cycles are very evident in sectors such as fashion, where there are spring-summer and autumn-winter seasons.

The events where the collections for the autumn-winter season will be launched are held more than six months in advance in order to cover the entire seasonality that includes the selection of pieces, the placing of orders, the shipping, its reception and its timely placement on shelves and showcases at the stores.

A mistake that can be deadly for an event is scheduling it during the most active or saturated dates for the participants, for example, planning a professional gift trade show in December; precisely the season in which the main exhibitors are focused on the marketing and delivery of products.

Before setting a date for your event, make sure you have verified with several of the main participants what availability of dates they have and be sure to learn to detail the sales cycle of the sector.

Sponsorships and Participating Companies

*"Whenever you see a successful business,
someone once made a courageous decision"*
PETER DRUCKER

Anchor Companies (Bellwethers)

The bellwether companies are those companies that provoke confidence in the attendees and that support the quality of the event; are those companies that generally act as sponsors or have a larger or more prominent space within the event.

If we think of a shopping center, we can emulate this concept; the prestigious department stores are the anchor businesses on which small businesses and specialized stores are amalgamated; in the same way, in a trade show or commercial area of a congress or convention, the bellwethers are those companies located at the front of the show floor around which small booths are distributed seeking the proximity of these leading companies.

My recommendation is to always start the marketing of an event seeking to obtain the largest number of anchor companies, detecting the real interest of the leaders to participate in your event will give you the certainty that you are on the right track.

Additionally, when you market or present your event with the endorsement of leading companies, either as participants or sponsors, it generates a cascading effect giving certainty and confidence to small and medium-sized participants, who will feel "sheltered" by the bellwethers.

"Seed" Companies

No less relevant is the participation of companies that I call "seed-companies". These are companies that, not being current leaders in the market, have all the potential to become leaders in the future and not only that, many of them will achieve this goal, due to their participation in your event.

They are generally small or medium-sized companies that have not yet managed to position themselves as leaders in the sector or that are recently created, but that have sufficient vision to know that participating in events in their sector will make them known and strengthen their perception among visitors and potential clients.

Supporting these companies is essential for event organizers; It is thanks to these companies that your event can be repeated in the future, if you achieve a critical mass of seed companies that become faithful to it and will support its different editions.

All companies start small, therefore our event, in addition to the support of consolidated companies, must always include and support startups and small participants who will in the future be our most loyal customers.

Sponsors

Sponsors are those companies that seek to spotlight their presence within our event, they are generally the first customers that we should approach at the beginning of the marketing and sales stage.

Sponsors are a very important source of income for events, in some cases they are basically the only source of income and therefore marketing strategies must be carefully designed for them; In general, the benefits granted to a sponsor must allow the brand to achieve a strong connection with the attendees, which needs to be visible at different stages of the event and through different technologies.

The ideal way to approach a brand is developing a "Sponsorship Plan", this plan can be designed in two ways:

The first one is to design "Sponsorship Packages", where a series of attractive benefits will be enumerated and that increase or decrease according to the cost and level of sponsorship.

The second, is by directly discussing with the sponsoring company what the goals and objectives are, to put together an "à la carte" package with the benefits that best suit the brand.

Types of event sponsorships:

Media Sponsors: sponsors who due to their essence or contacts, can ensure a promotion and presence of our event in the media through interviews or mentions on their social networks.

Cash Sponsorship: sponsors who pay to have their brand presence or activations at the event through a sponsorship contract.

In-kind Sponsorship: brands or companies that donate or give products or services instead of paying with cash.

Promotion partners: influencers, celebrities or public figures who promote our event to their followers or fan base.

The Attendee

"Come as a guest and leave as a friend,
We´re in the business of making memories"
JO DAVIS

The attendee is our reason for being, events are designed for and by people.

The hospitality industry's foundation is the service, our events industry is strongly inserted in hospitality, that is how its essence is also based on service, the satisfaction of everyone who attends is the core of our reason for being.

Attendee values

All those attending an event have a series of values that distinguish them, these values largely define their tastes and their actions, therefore, whenever we hold an event, we must ask ourselves: What are the values that define my attendee?

Values change over time and they are the result of different influences on the person: their family education, the religion they profess, personal or family beliefs, mentors and guides, in addition to important events that transform their point of view.

If we design a medical convention, we can recognize that there are intrinsic values of a doctor that define the attendees and therefore are related to them, for example: honesty & ethics.

If you are able to identify these values and manage to use them, you will achieve an event that is in tune with the attendees, you will also have very specific ideas for activities and activations.

A practical way is to list the five most important values that you consider as the defining values of your target audience, in the case of an event for motorcyclists, the design of the campaign, the materials and the conceptualization of the activations and shows are always linked to the values that are the axes of the motorcycle community; values like:
1) Brotherhood
2) Solidarity
3) Freedom
4) Independence
5) Adventure

From these five values, the organizing committee begins to develop ideas related to the use of certain colors that reflect these values and that serve as the basis for the design of the image and media campaign.

Activations and shows are tied to these values, either as a whole or highlighting one in particular, to achieve a consistency between the rider's lifestyle, his vision of the world and the environment in which he identifies himself consciously and unconsciously.

Generations and new consumer groups.

It is not new to anyone that the evolution of humanity has been marked by social, demographic, political and historical events that define entire generations. These generations are intertwined and today they coexist forming a range of tastes and ways of thinking and living.
As event designers we need to learn about these generational defining characteristics and use them as our guide.

Currently we have several generations as attendees to professional events: Generation "X" born between 1965 and 1979, Millennials born between 1980 and 2000 and Generation "Z" born between 2001 and 2010.

There is a large bibliography related to the characteristics of each of these generations, so in this book we will limit ourselves to emphasize the importance of holding events that may be attractive to specific audiences and also events that are inclusive for more than one generation.

We can say that the younger a generation is, the event should be more inclusive, it should help the audience become part of it; not only by attending, but by actively participating in its development.

The congresses where people must sit for hours listening to the speakers and the trade shows where you will practically go through corridors like in a museum, are losing attractiveness in front of generations that demand inclusion, freedom of expression and prominence.

Design your event based on the characteristics of your attendee, get to know him thoroughly and consider his behaviors, desires, cover his expectations and seek the creation of new experiences where year after year the attendee finds a reflection not only of the industry or sector of the event, but also a space that reflects the feelings of that generation.

New generational groups have recently joined consumer groups that share interests and tastes; These new consumers are always on the move and are more linked to a lifestyle or "tribe" than to an age; Among them we can mention: extended families, runners, same sex couples, pet lovers, foodies and healthy life consumers, all of them with unique characteristics and tastes.

Local customs and traditions

Local customs are essential in the design of an event, since it is through their deep knowledge that we can design an event that is truly compatible with the attendees; You must be aware that it is these traditions and customs that largely define the protocol that will govern the symbolic and ceremonial moments in a wedding or an inauguration in a congress or trade show.

For the inauguration of an event related to the packaging industry in the U.S., it was decided to make a tour of the corridors of the trade show with a war band, while in the Mexican version of the same trade show, the tour was performed with a mariachi band.

The success of different types of business events also depends on the country, in the United States an early breakfast for the press or for an executive meeting works very well, while in Spain the ideal is to make a cocktail in the afternoon.

When putting together a presidium table we must consider the precedence that is customary in that industry or country.

Dress code

The dress code refers to the type and style of clothing in which it is considered correct to dress for an event; Although this topic is of greater weight in social events, communicating the correct dress code in a professional or corporate event is the responsibility of the organizer, it must be announced promptly on each invitation and must be included in the activities program.

The dress code should be consistent with the corporate image of the company and to a greater extent with the type of event that is taking place, there are different styles and it is important to understand that any event should be linked to the essence of the business; For example, technology companies tend to have a "natural" style that defines a less strict use of corporate suits or clothing; instead, a bank tends to have a "traditional" style.

This is how corporate events should reinforce the essence of the corporation. These styles can be transferred to the institutional or corporate image and based on it we can develop the decoration design, determine the dress code and even the menu.

To define the type of clothing you can use the following guide:

Informal: based on simplicity, naturalness, comfort.

Business attire: it is the most frequently used in events, a dark suit and tie is recommended for men and for women a cocktail dress.

Etiquette: mostly used in gala events, very formal events or if you are hosting an event, for men it is recommended to wear white tie, black tie or tuxedo, for women it is a long dress or evening dress.

Beach or warm weather destinations: the ideal is to use fabrics such as linen, chambray or cotton for both men and women.

International Visitors

All countries have a strong potential for holding international events; the participation of international attendees is one of the most valuable opportunities of promotion for any country; therefore, knowing the cultural differences and cultural needs of our international visitors allows us to incorporate into the event the elements that are a sign of our interest in hosting them.

Consider and respect mealtimes, prayer time, even proxemic (accepted proximity space with our interlocutor). If we use any "icebreaker" activity between different nationalities, including a more intimate approach such as hugs, it will be well received in Latin cultures; however, if there are individuals from Asian countries within our group, this exercise will be considered inappropriate for a business topic.

When hosting events with international participants, be sure to learn a little about their culture before scheduling and designing activities and activations.

Companions

Some events allow someone who is not necessarily a direct delegate to participate as guest; these guests are generally relatives or companions of our attendee; their successful participation and evaluation of the event is a determining factor in our success.

When designing a congress or convention program, it is imperative to design a guest program considering the free time that the conference attendees will have during the different programs and ideally we should tie these times with the guest program so that both, the guest and the attendee, participate in the integration events and social activities; If we have a DMC working with us, he will provide multiple options of activities, thanks to its destination local expertise.

Conference Design and its Content

"It usually takes three weeks to prepare an improvised speech"
MARK TWAIN

Conferences represent the core part of a congress or convention; in addition, some trade shows and corporate events include a cycle of conferences as part of the event offer.

Selecting the right conferences to be presented in a program is a challenge that we must take to detail, and we most make sure it will be a success.

The idea is to always be purposeful and to anticipate what is already being discussed in the sector.

There are two key sources from which we can draw ideas, the first and most important are the leading companies; These are our first source of information, they will also be the first interested in making known what they consider most attractive to their clients and even to their competition.

Ideally, we should negotiate their participation by offering the possibility to sponsor a conference, including the travel allowance and the speaker´s fee.

Another source of information for conference topics, is direct research or "trend hunting", we can start our research through the Internet or by contacting the associations and organizations that are related with the topics of our interest, if possible, we should appoint interviews with the executives and actors who are defining the directions of the industry for which we will hold the event. The more innovative and updated the program, the more interest and profitability we will achieve.

Food and Beverages

"Food is our common ground, a universal experience"
JAMES BEARD

There are several elements that contribute to achieving a unique experience for event attendees, however, food is undoubtedly one of the most relevant.

During the different meal moments, those attending the event put into action each of their senses, in addition to connecting with each other, making this moment highly memorable.

The first consideration we must acknowledge is the size of the event, we can use the following information to size our event appropriately:

Small event: 2 - 200 attendees

Medium size event: 200 to 500 attendees

Large event: 500 to 1,000 attendees

Mega event: more than 1000 attendees

Catering service companies must be able to provide budgets based on these numbers.

An event traditionally involves food service, it can be a full menu service, a coffee break, sandwiches, box lunch, canapés, cocktail, etc.

Classic Menu
5 items
Side dish, starter, soup, main course, and dessert.

Modern Menu
4 items
Side dish, starter, main course, and dessert.
Entrees, soup, main course, and dessert.
Starter, soup, main course, and dessert.

Contemporary Menu
3 items
Starters, main course, and dessert.
Side dish, main course, and dessert.

Tasting menu
It is a menu with several food options consisting of five or more dishes and with smaller meal portions than normal.

Menus are design based on the main course, this dish defines the characteristics of the rest of the dishes on the menu in terms of portions, quality category and flavors.

Currently there are different trends in food and gastronomy, in addition there are attendees who have special requirements (kosher, vegan, celiac, etc.). Our main objective is to provide a menu that suits the budget and style of our event:

Gourmet - emphasis on the quality and sophistication of the ingredients.

Artisan - traditional food prepared with endemic products of the region.

Organic - food based on the commitment to the environment.

Biodynamic - food harvested respecting the moon phases and without chemical fertilizers.

Vegan – a menu that refrains from the use of products of animal origin.

International food - is a menu made with the influence and gastronomy from different countries.

Fusion - menu that mixes culinary styles from different cultures.

We also have specific food trends for events like:

- *Finger Food* - bites of food for individual consumption
- *Junk Bar* – a candy and snack bar with a fun presentation.
- *Show cooking* - preparing dishes and drinks live in front of the guests.
- *Guest Chef* - invite a chef to design the menu creating the interest of diners and the media.

- *Pop Up gastronomy* - celebration of tastings in alternative spaces such as wineries, galleries, or museums.

If we celebrate our event in a venue that was not "born" for events; For example, a vineyard or a local park, the food service tends to be more expensive in around +20%, given the adaptations that will have to be made to achieve a quality service.

Ideally go and visit the venue in the season and the hour that the event will take place to find out the temperature conditions that will affect the food service and take the necessary precautions.

Menu Design

The engineering of a menu implies the consideration of different factors such as the formality and character of the event, whether the food will be served indoors or outdoors, the temperature of the place, the season of the year, seasonal products and various other factors, It is more practical to receive advice from the F&B area of the premises, or from the catering company and trust their experience to have an optimal menu, it is always advisable to ask the supplier for a tasting menu, to become familiar with the plating and serving.

Wines and Spirits

The ideal complement to food is drink, knowing how to choose the type of drink, as well as making the purchase properly, will help to successfully complete the menu.

There are two types of alcoholic beverages, fermented and distilled.

Fermented beverages are mainly wine, beer, sake, and other regional drinks.

The wines are usually classified as table wines, sparkling wines, fortified wines, and flavored wines (vermouths) and their prestige and cost largely depend on the wine region where their grapes come from.

Its leading role in events is relevant and since there is a great variety in qualities and prices, there are multiple options to select a very good wine at a good price, the ideal is to contact suppliers or importers and build loyalty with them so that they become our trusted suppliers.

Beers are fermented alcoholic beverages made from barley malt or other cereals flavored with hops. Its role in corporate and professional events is more limited, however, the rise of craft beer has positioned this drink as a different option and with greater "status".

Distilled beverages can be classified into spirits and liqueurs, spirits are dry alcohols with low sugar content and liqueurs are sweet alcohols thanks to the addition of sugar.

The distilled spirits or drinks are classified by the main ingredient, the grape distillates are: Cognac, Armagnac, Brandy, the grain distillates are: Whiskey, Vodka and Geneva, cane distillate: Rum, potato distillate: Aquavit and agave distillates: Tequila and Mezcal.

Drinks without alcohol

A good design of a menu of non-alcoholic drinks can make a big difference in an event, generally these soft drinks tend to be the same everywhere.

There is a growing trend to offer low-calorie, healthy food and drinks. Alternative non-alcoholic drinks are an ideal option to stand out and be purposeful.

Non-alcoholic drinks are traditionally juices, lemonades, oranges, and carbonated drinks (soft drinks); however, more elaborate and personality non-alcoholic beverages known as "mocktails" have recently emerged.

The mocktail is the fusion of two English words, "mock" and "cocktail", and its meaning would be "a cocktail simulation", that is, a non-alcoholic cocktail.

These drinks are ideal for giving event guests a creative and purposeful choice, these drinks can be designed to reflect the corporate or institutional colors of the company.

Detox waters, fruit smoothies, smoothies and immune system boosters are also trending.

Alcohols calculation

Wine

For the calculation of the wine performance, we must consider that wine bottles usually contain 750 ml, therefore, the wine yield will depend directly on the size of the glass of wine that is used in the event.

In a 12-ounce glass, 4oz (120 mL) should be served, therefore the yield is 6.25 glasses per bottle of wine.

5.33oz (160 mL) should be served in a 16-ounce glass, so the yield is 4.7 glasses per bottle of wine.

6oz (180mL) should be served in an 18-ounce glass so the yield is 4.1 glasses per bottle of wine.

Decimals are important in performance as at large events these will turn into full bottles.

To calculate the necessary bottles according to the type of event, at lunches and dinners two glasses of wine should be considered for each diner, in cocktail-type events two glasses of wine should be considered for each hour of the event.

Spirits and Liquors

To calculate the performance of distillates and spirits, considering again a 750-milliliter bottle, the performance will depend on the type of service we are providing, common service or open bar.

In common service, 1.5 oz (45 mL) must be served per glass, each yield is 16.66 services.

Open bar should serve 1 oz (30 mL) per glass or cup, therefore, the yield is 25 services.

Environmental Design

"Design is so simple, that's why it is so complicated"
PAUL RAND

The environmental design of an event is of crucial importance, it must be taken care of in every detail, not only considering the thematic characteristics of the event, but also the physical characteristics of the venue and the profile of our attendee.

The spaces psychologically influence the mood of the attendees, in addition to stimulating their senses. Each decoration element we use, must reinforce the message and intention of each defined moment within the timeline of the event.

Color

Color is one of the most powerful tools for influencing moods, warm colors or cold colors can be used and thus provoke the emotions we desire, color can help us stimulate or reassure our attendees.

The use of colors in events:

Blue - promotes calm and serenity, increases productivity, ideal for academic events, conferences, and business meetings.

Red - increases heartbeat and breathing, is bright warm and evokes strong, sensual emotions. It is used in social events, sports events, and product presentations.

Green - symbolizes nature, gives tranquility, and represents health, ideal for social or family events.

White - represents goodness, purity, and innocence, it is ideal for corporate and luxury events.

Black - is used in events that need to convey elegance, sobriety, and formality.

Music

There is no important moment in social rites or special moments in the life of a person without music, its correct selection and use will ensure unforgettable moments and the cohesion of all attendees.

Music stimulates the functions of both hemispheres of the brain in addition to stimulating the production of dopamine; It can regulate our body motor activity either to calm or stress our body.

Music also causes our body to try to match our breathing and our heartbeats with the rhythm of music, becoming a powerful tool that we can use to modify the mood or highlight a specific moment.

If the volume of the music exceeds 95 decibels, our physical and mental reaction capacity is reduced by up to 20%.

It is our responsibility to monitor the decibels to achieve a harmonious interaction between the participants of corporate events and avoid diminishing their reaction capacity.

A correct selection of music can literally make the event unforgettable, as the music stimulates the hypothalamus largely responsible for long-term memory.

When designing an event, do not forget to:
Define the "environments" that must be created through music and what is the state of mind that is required to choose the type of music for each of those moments.

Create a "playlist" for each mood; Share it and discuss it with your client, in any event it is imperative to be aware of how the audience is reacting to the music and modify it if necessary.

Make sure that the volume for each space is adequate and that it allows interaction and conversation between attendees.

Lighting

Natural light lowers stress levels and promotes the body's natural cycles, making it the most recommended type of light for educational and professional events.

When an inspection visit is made to a venue, we must pay attention to the type of lighting in each of the spaces, it is always advisable to request that the lights be turned on, especially if the space does not have natural light.

In addition, we must consider that artificial light changes colors depending on its hue, whether it is hot or cold and that a decorative element can change radically based on the type of light used.

Lighting is ideal when we want to highlight an object or person, we may use precise lights that highlight the product to be launched or the company president, lighting can also be used to highlight building facades, hall entrances and create high impact effects.

Artificial light, on the other hand, is stimulating and alters the circadian cycle. This causes physical and mental changes in the attendees, it is extremely important to consider which are the moments of the event that will benefit from artificial light, and which from natural light to accordingly create the right environments.

Temperature

A determining factor to truly enjoy an event is the temperature of the room, especially as event organizers when choosing a venue we must consider that weather conditions may change depending on the time of the day, it is not the same to visit a garden or any open space by day or by night.

Preferably we must make the inspection visit at the same time as the event will take place, in order to have a real and clear idea of the lighting and temperature that we will have on the day of the event.

The temperature of the place also influences the dress code to be used and we must make the appropriate dressing recommendations so that attendees enjoy the event to the fullest.

Aromas

The use of aromas is highly effective since it is the stimulus that rises the fastest to the brain. It also serves to reinforce the category of a business... a cafeteria smells like coffee or even to identify a brand, through olfactory marketing, we can generate strong emotional bonds with the attendee.

It is generally used by placing devices such as nebulizers that serve to perfume the event areas; However, the scents should not be chosen at random since each scent has different effects and, like music, it can create a feeling of peace or raise the spirits of the audience.

For example; smells like vanilla, coffee or chocolate help bring home memories and generally have a relaxing effect, woody smells are more elegant and manly, the aromas like strawberry or lavender tend to be feminine while citrus smells like lemon or orange can be used in more informal events while mint for conferences and events where it is required to increase the concentration of the attendees.

If the use of the aroma is excessive, this will be unpleasant to the audience, so my recommendation is to contact an olfactory marketing expert that can advise you on the selection of an aroma or on the design of a unique aroma that is distinctive of your brand or event.

Sanitary measures

Health considerations include all those measures that protect the health of attendees, there are regulations that apply in any physical space where a large number of people gather and that are established by country, geographic region or even by city, make sure you know them before making any massive summons.

Some of the most recurring measures in accessing events are the use of sanitation tunnels, body temperature readers, as well as the prior and subsequent disinfection of spaces.

In food and beverages, the constant supervision of food preparation processes, as well as the sanitation of production areas and the obtaining of safety certificates are some of the constant requirements for event organizers.

Choosing a Destination

"There's not a country that I´ve visited I haven't fallen in love with... "

Influence zone

All host cities have a perfectly defined "zone of influence", this zone of influence is intrinsically linked to its location and the communication channels that allow access to it; Traditionally, a city is considered to have a zone of influence delimited by a circumference that covers three hundred kilometers from any point to its downtown or center.

The zone of influence of the city of Frankfurt in Germany, includes those surrounding cities located in that radius of influence: Munich, Cologne, Prague, Paris and Brussels.

Considering the area of influence allows us to have a clear idea of the geographical area from which it will be easier to have visitors, due to its proximity. It also allows us to prepare a promotion plan that seeks to generate greater impact in the natural area of influence of the venue or, to reinforce with specific strategies in locations that are not part of this area of influence, but that are very important for the event.

The area of influence can also be applied to countries, especially in places such as Europe or Central and South America where there are some countries with a medium or small territorial extension and whose area of influence of three hundred kilometers includes several countries.

Connectivity

The connectivity of the city is another factor that strongly influences the success of an event since it represents the ease with which attendees can travel by land, rail or air to the destination,

Before selecting any destination we must prepare a chart where we must specify the travel connections as well as the schedules of each of these means of transportation, as well as a table of distances from the destination to the main neighboring cities, additionally to the travel time by car.

The travel costs to the chosen destination are also a determining factor, on one occasion we decided to hold an event in a port destination that seemed totally suitable with the theme of the congress; However, the result was not as expected since there were flights only three days a week and most of the attendees had to stop in Mexico City, which made their participation more expensive.

Destination Strengths

All destinations have a series of well-identified strengths due to their location, infrastructure, and personality; these strengths are the destination essence and the reason why it can distinguish from other destinations.

Several cities have worked on slogans and positioned hashtags and phrases that highlight their main qualities, perfectly defining the character of the place.

A clear example of this is the city of Las Vegas, Nevada in the USA. This city is characterized by launching a marketing campaign each season that reinforces its character as a city of fun, excesses, shows and more recently gastronomy.

Ideally when selecting a destination, it is important to ensure that we have a balance in: the ideal facilities for our event, leisure attractions for our attendees and their companions, in addition to a varied gastronomic offer both in price and range.

Limitations of a Destination

There are also limitations on destinations, returning to the example of the city of Las Vegas, its natural vocation is ideal for leisure and business events, but is probably an unfavorable environment for family or religious events.

Other limitations have to do with safety and connectivity, which we have previously discussed.

Leisure & Attractions

Having a destination attractive enough on its own to invite attendees to enjoy, is an advantage that will play in our favor and that will also give us the opportunity to include activations for both attendees and their companions.

Safety

Safety refers to the possibility or not of situations that endanger the integrity of the attendees; This condition is linked to the political situation of the country or city and its ability to maintain public order; in addition to other variables such as the possibility of infections, food contamination, epidemics and natural disasters.

Venue Selection

The Space

Every space is designed to generate emotional (chemical) reactions in our brains that predispose us to feel in harmony or uncomfortable with it. This is because a space is made up of materials, lighting, geometric elements, and colors, among other factors.

When we select the venue for our event, we must review the objectives that we wish to achieve and ensure that the space gives us, in a natural way the sensations that we wish to convey or, consider what adaptations (for example, lighting) we must implement to communicate them; these adjustments will in most cases become an additional expense in our budget.

An interesting exercise is to ask yourself: How does this space makes me feel? Welcome? Comfortable? Do I feel oppressed? Protected?

For example, a garden makes us feel good since it connects with nature and gives us a feeling of spaciousness, natural lighting, and general well-being, therefore, its identity is ideal for family events.

In contrast, a cave generates a feeling of confinement, intimacy, and low light; therefore, it becomes the ideal space for a cocktail or a more intimate corporate event.

Prestige

Each venue has a certain status, this status is the result of a constant quality service that creates a reputation, it is imperative to know the standing of the place that we are going to use, if the prestige is solid, it is most likely precisely because of this that we have decided to make our event in that place; On the contrary, if it is a space that we do not know, it is very useful to request the references of two or three clients, to be able to request their testimonials.

As in any event, congruence is the first characteristic of a successful event, if we organize a luxury event in a three-star hotel, this inconsistency will be reflected in the quality of the visitors, in the same way an event aimed at an open audience, held in a space with the perception of being expensive or inaccessible will cause us to have few visitors.

Capacity

It is the extent of the space to comfortably accommodate the expected number of attendees, it is advisable to ensure that the space can not only accommodate the number of attendees, but also that it will not forcefully exceed that number and that the event doesn´t appears empty.

The venue staff generally knows to detail their facilities and can recommend different ways of distribution allowing us to prevent our event from looking lackluster, they also know how to accommodate both furniture and decoration to avoid it.

The capacities of a space depend directly on the selected distribution: auditorium, banquet, cocktail, or school; you can make calculations of the number of people as follows:

Auditorium: 0.85 m per person. (2.8 feet)

Banquet setting:
a. Table for 8 people, 1.45 m per person. (4.7 feet)
b. Table for 10 people, 1.20 m per person. (4 feet)
c. Table for 12 people, 1 m per person. (3.2 feet)

Cocktail setup: 0.90 m per person. (3 feet)

Classroom setup:
a. Half table 1.42 m per person. (4.5 feet)
b. Full table 1.20 m per person. (4 feet)

In the case of trade shows and fairs, the calculation of the total space is made through the number of nine meters booths (3m X 3m) that can be housed in that space, additionally it is necessary to increase 50% more space, which will be the space required for corridors, common areas and services.

Safety

Safety is very dependable of the event distribution, but also to the architectural and structural design of the contracted space.

In any inspection visit to the site, we must ask for the location of emergency exits, fire extinguishers, evacuation routes and meeting points in case of an emergency, as well as if there is any civil protection program.

It is imperative to take a tour of these areas, locate them and make sure that our staff knows them and knows what to do in the event of an unforeseen event. Many public and private spaces are obliged to have internal civil protection brigades, we must know if they exist. and have a prior coordination meeting with them.

Rules and Regulations

All professional venues have an internal document called "Rules and Regulations", this regulations allows the organizers to know if there are restrictions related mainly to the use of the physical space and particularly at the time of the event move-in.

A clear example is the impossibility of making paint finishes in fairgrounds or the use of flammable substances, the use of drones and other restrictions that in most cases have their roots in civil protection and in the proper use of the facilities based on the venue height specifications, floor strength, etc.

Ease of Move-In and Move-Out

One element that can impact our budget is the ease of setting up and dismantling the event.

If the space we have chosen does not have enough loading and unloading platforms or the forklifts are not enough to receive our exhibitors or suppliers, this means more time and therefore more money invested.

Usually venues charge per day or 12-hour shifts, one possibility to avoid this additional cost is to negotiate with the venue, that the installation and dismantling hours have a preferential cost.

Insurance

Most venues have an insurance that covers all incidents that may happen within the property; however, you must consider an additional insure after reviewing and discussing with the venue what is and what is not included in theirs.

Negotiations with the Venue

The venue becomes the "home" of our event. For the visitor, both - event and venue - coexist in an inseparable symbiosis. One of our best relationships should be with the venue, remember that the organization of events is full of special requirements and having the unconditional support of the venue executives, is imperative for our success.

Negotiations must always be clear and in writing, especially any special concessions that we have achieved in the contracting negotiations, since generally the person who sells the premises to us is not the person who operates at the show floor, and there may be differences of opinion that if not detailed in the contract may be invalidated by one of the parties.

We should express our requirements with absolute freedom and clarity, since our objective is to achieve a win-win negotiation, and as organizers we are the raison d'être of the venues.

Event Layout

"Everything fits in a little jar, if you know how to accommodate it"
MEXICAN PROVERB

We have already discussed on how each space has a natural vocation that allows us to take advantage of its characteristics, an essential part of our work as organizers is to work on an efficient and optimal distribution of these spaces.

It is important to consider in all event distribution the location of emergency exits, hydrants and be aware that the distribution must always protect the physical integrity of the people who will participate in the event.

This takes on special relevance in fairgrounds and convention centers since these generally receive the visit of the civil protection area of their locality, these agents visit the events regularly to ensure that the pre-established rules for these spaces are being complied with, and with the forecasts delivered and declared directly and previously by the organizer to the authority.

Remember that emergency meeting points and evacuation directions should be made known to attendees, ideally at the start of the event, as well as having proper signage at key locations.

We can choose different types of emplacements to organize an event. Below, I present the most common arrangements for events: (go to page 74)

Auditorium: the seats are arranged emulating a theater.

Banquet: the places are arranged around round tables with capacities of 8, 10 or 12 people; in some occasions the "crescent" sit-in is used, which consists of occupying only half of the seats available at the round table, thus allowing greater visibility when making a visual presentation or when there is a presidium.

Classroom: Seats are arranged in rows with tables to facilitate writing and placement of materials to be used during the event.

Horseshoe: Tables are arranged forming letters (U, E or T) and the sitting places for the attendees are arranged around them, this arrangement seeks to provoke greater interaction between all attendees.

Russian Table: A square is formed with the tables, placing the chairs around, leaving an empty space in the center; It is an ideal setting for corporate events where the interaction of the attendees is sought to be equitable.

Free seating: the seating arrangement does not follow any specific accommodation; creativity is the rule.

In the case of some conventions and congresses, it is customary to integrate a commercial area or mini-trade show as part of the event, in which case its position must be strategically located so that the attendees can visit it during the coffee breaks.

In the case of the trade shows, the distribution is planned mainly under the logic of commercialization, that is, the booths are distributed so that sales are easier.

Leading companies booths are usually located in the front row or at the entrance of the trade show, however, my recommendation is to look for a distribution that allows different areas of interest and flow of visitors to prevent subsequent areas from losing interest and being more difficult to sell. One idea is to place activations or convince anchor companies to locate in these areas in exchange for some benefit granted by us.

In product presentations, press conferences and any corporate event it is important to have designated areas for important clients, high-ranking executives and specialized press; this way we will ensure that VIP attendees can appreciate and enjoy the event to the fullest.

Associations and Organizations

"If you walk alone, you will go faster
If you walk accompanied, you will go further"
AFRICAN PROVERB

Every event frequently requires the support of associations or institutions, for example, if we hold a medical congress, ideally having the endorsement of the ministry or secretary of health, will give confidence to the attendees.

Generally, in an trade show, congress or convention, there are two types of related organizations to which we must approach, the first type refers to those organizations or associations, which have to do with exhibitors.

For example: "National Association of Urban Furniture Manufacturers", the second type refers to those who have to do with the attendees, for example: "National Association of Urban Planners".

When we devise a corporate event, one of the first steps to take is to visit these organizations.

During these visits we will have the opportunity to learn more about the sector, probably to obtain statistics and databases, and we will also be able to know the problematics and trends that are affecting that industry.

A favorable negotiation can be to give prominence to the association or organism in our event, showing its logo in the promotional material and in the training or working materials on site.

It is also convenient to ask them as part of the presidium in our inaugurations or press conferences.

Another organization that can support the promotion of your event is the CVB (convention and visitor bureau), which has among its main functions and interests precisely to promote its city; Contact these offices and most likely you will get promotional supports at no cost.

The greater the number of attendees at your event, the greater the possibility the CVB will help you promote the event, since it will join efforts to achieve a greater economic impact in that city.

It is also a good interlocutor with collateral entities such as hotels, restaurants and in general all those establishments that benefit from the visit of tourists to the city and also to prepare a joint plan that benefits everyone including the itinerary for the pre or post congress.

Other benefits that can be obtained through the CVB are:
• Promotional material of the city.
• Inspection visits.

- Sponsorship of VIP guests and speakers.
- Discount or free transportation for participants within the city.

Marketing and Public Relations.

"Marketing is no longer about the stuff that you make but about the stories you tell"
SETH GODIN

An indisputable ally in the promotion of events are the mass media, the specialized media and the social networks; each has different potential to inform our attendees of what is relevant to that group, and they are our natural allies before and after the event.

Mass media such as television and radio continue to be part of a good promotional mix especially if the event is aimed to the general public; Even movie theaters are an excellent option to consider, we recently used them in one of our events and it worked very well.

There are television channels and radio stations with a very defined and clear segmentation, taking advantage of this is essential to have a successful impact, investment in these media is expensive and the ideal way to have a positive impact is through a detailed analysis of the audience to tie it with our attendees.

Social media continues to grow in importance and is now a fundamental tool to reach our target audience.
Segmentation is a must and the correct use of the appropriate visual and verbal language for each media must be carefully designed.

Each of the channels and networks speak their own language and therefore the graphic production and campaign conceptualization must be carried out for each one in particular, mainly considering the age of the group; For example, Facebook is often more used by young people and adults, while Instagram, Tik Tok and YouTube have a greater influence on adolescents and children.

The key words for success in the social networks are consistency and quality of content, maintaining the demand for quality content is a challenge and responsibility for those who manage the networks of our event.

Once we have defined the media, we will proceed to design a promotion and marketing plan that lists the chosen channels and that defines month after month the actions and intensity of the campaign; my recommendation is to intensify the promotion at least three months in advance.

This promotion plan is vital not only to be clear about how we are going to publicize the event, but also to show our sponsors, exhibitors, and clients what we will do to attract our visitors.

The use of influencers is relatively a new alternative, they tend to be more useful to reach younger audiences and their tone is generally inclined towards humor; Every day they grow more in importance and this makes their hiring more expensive. It is crucial to be sure that we choose someone who really benefits our brand and is compatible with our values.

Another major task is to develop a public relations plan that allows us create an ideal relationship and communication with clients, partners, employees, government and the media; it starts by defining clear and strong lines of communication that will help emphasize the characteristics of the event, in addition to highlighting how the event contributes to the industry to which it belongs

These lines of communication will be used in official communications, press releases and in interviews; Along with the creation of these lines of communication, spokespersons must be appointed to help elevate them.

The spokespersons may belong to our organization, or they may be opinion leaders of organizations, chambers or industry associations that have agreed to support the event, give interviews on our behalf, and/or participate in press conferences.

Budget

Rule number 1: never lose money.
Rule number 2: never forget rule number 1"
WARREN BUFFETT

Budget is not always the part that event planners like to develop the most, however, it is through the budget analysis that we can ground our ideas so that they can be a reality.

The budget does not have to be complicated. It is a fact that each type of event has its peculiarities, but as you run more and more events you can adapt the budget concepts without difficulty.

The budget should be designed once we are clear about the type of event we want to organize, as well as when the destination, the venue and all the activities of the program are defined.

Income

List all those concepts that will become a benefit in money or kind, the most common concepts related to an event income are:

- Conference program (congress, convention) - amount paid by the attendees to attend conferences.

- Special events or activations - amount paid by the sponsoring companies for on the show activations.

- Trade show floor - amount derived from the sale of booths at a trade show.

- Box Office - amount obtained from ticket sales.

- Sponsorships - amount paid by companies that invest an amount of money to promote their brand or product within our event.

- Exchanges - is the value of the products or benefits exchanged with any brand or supplier.

- Financial gains - are those gains derived from the financial returns obtained from the investment of income. An event generally receives income before it takes place, in some cases these incomes are attractive enough to be invested in some financial instrument such as promissory notes or investment funds and thus produce an additional profit.

- Exchange rate gains - Some events receive the registration fees or the payment of booths in a different currency than the one used locally.

There are two frequently used options, fix the exchange rate of the currency for the clients to pay us, or use the exchange rate of the day they paid us , when making the accounting closing of the event we will know if the exchange rate affected us during the time we were receiving these payments and if we were able to obtain an economic benefit, derived from the fluctuation of our currency against the other.

Expenses

Fixed expenses of the event are those that do not vary in relation to the number of attendees, for example, audiovisual equipment, venue costs, promotion, and advertising, etc.

Variable expenses are those which do depend on the number of attendees: meals, folders, giveaways and the working material for the congress or convention etc.

In a product presentation cocktail, it corresponds to the quantity of canapés and drinks requested. In the case of an trade show, variable expenses will correspond, for example, to the number of booths to be produced, the greater the number of booths, the greater the expense on equipment, but it also means a higher income from booth sales.

A very important part of the budget is the one related to the supplier's payments, my recommendation is to develop a directory of suppliers by selecting two or three for each category based on the quality of their service.

The main expenses related to suppliers are:

- Audio and video.

- Promotion and hostess agencies.

- Banquets. (catering)

- Decoration.

- Design and booth construction.

- Musical groups.

- Lighting.

- Translation services.

- Transportation or land operator.

- Communication technologies.

As we mentioned earlier, make sure you have contact with two or three companies in each of these categories and work to forge a win-win relationship with each of them.

Since we have calculated the variable expenses and the fixed expenses together, we will have the total expenses, this number is used to calculate the cost per conventioneer or participant.

Example:

If our fixed expenses have an amount of US $ 150,000.00 and our variable expense per person is $ 90 dollars, estimating an attendance of 400 participants we would have:

$ 150,000.00 + $ 36,000 ($ 90 X 400) = $ 186,000.00 / 400 = US $ 465.00

Therefore, our sale price for each participant should be greater than this figure, now, if our estimated profit percentage is for example 25%, then we would already have the desired income:

Total expenses $ 186,000.00 X 25% = US $ 46,500 of expected profits.

Total desired income = $ 186,000 plus $ 46,500 = US $ 232,500.00

In this example, if we no longer had any additional income, the cost for each of the 400 participants should be: $ 232,500 / 400 = $ 582 dollars.

Do not forget to include in your budget, bank charges for credit card payments or bank transfers, and of course do not forget to consider 5% more for unforeseen expenses.

Remember that, if you are very clear about your expenses, you will have the possibility to better calculate the costs of your services and products, but above all you will have certainty about the correct sale price for your event.

Conclusions

Event design is undoubtedly a growing business; If you provide professional and practical tools to your staff and organization, you will obtain a competitive advantage that will give your clients the security of a more solid and successful event.

When designing your events, review the topics covered in this book; Use it to review each new project and adjust it, make sure this topics become a natural part of your analysis and can be reflected in a "Business Operation Plan".

The next step is to bring your ideas to reality; creativity and excellent service will give you the competitive advantage and differentiation that so many clients are looking for.

Welcome to the incredible world of events!

I wish you the best of success.

Glossary

A

Attendees - People who participate as active guests in the official program of the event.

B

Booth – Commercial area within an event, designed for the promotion or sale of products and services.

Briefing - Document that compiles in a schematic and short way the main characteristics of an event.

C

Capacity - Maximum authorized number of people that a venue can admit for shows or other public events.

Catering - Food and drink supply service at an event.

Ceremony - Said to do something, with all the apparatus and solemnity that corresponds to it.

Ceremonial - Series or set of formalities for any public or solemn act.

Civil Protection - System whose mission is to provide protection and assistance to the citizens of a country.

Cocktail - Event where cocktails are offered accompanied by light food and other drinks.

Coffee Break - Short break for activities, which generally includes the service of coffee, tea, water, and cookies.

Committee - Group of people responsible for the comprehensive operation of an event.

Companion - Person who travels with the event attendee, without participating in the official activities, conferences, and activations of the event.

D

Destination management company DMC - Private company that coordinates travel, meeting, entertainment and transportation services to individuals or groups in a destination of which they are specialists.

E
Exhibitor - Person or entity that occurs at a public trade show with objects of its property or industry for its promotion.

H
Hospitality - Good reception and welcome to foreigners, visitors, or participants of an event.

I
Influencer - Person who has credibility on a specific topic and who has a great presence and influence on social networks.

P

"Professional conference organizer" PCO - It is a person or company specialized in conference management.

Plan of the event - It is the document that reflects the distribution of the event generally to scale and with measurements.

Precedence -Preeminence or preference in the place and seat in some honorary acts such as inaugurations or press conferences.

Protocol - Set of rules established by norm or custom for ceremonies and official or solemn acts.

V
Venue - Building or generally closed space, where the event will take place.

S

"Sitting" - Distribution of seats. Floor plan or document showing where people should sit during an event.

Sponsor - Said of a person or entity: That sponsors an event frequently for advertising purposes.

Staff - Fixed or temporary staff, who are part of the organizing committee of the event

Event Setting Up

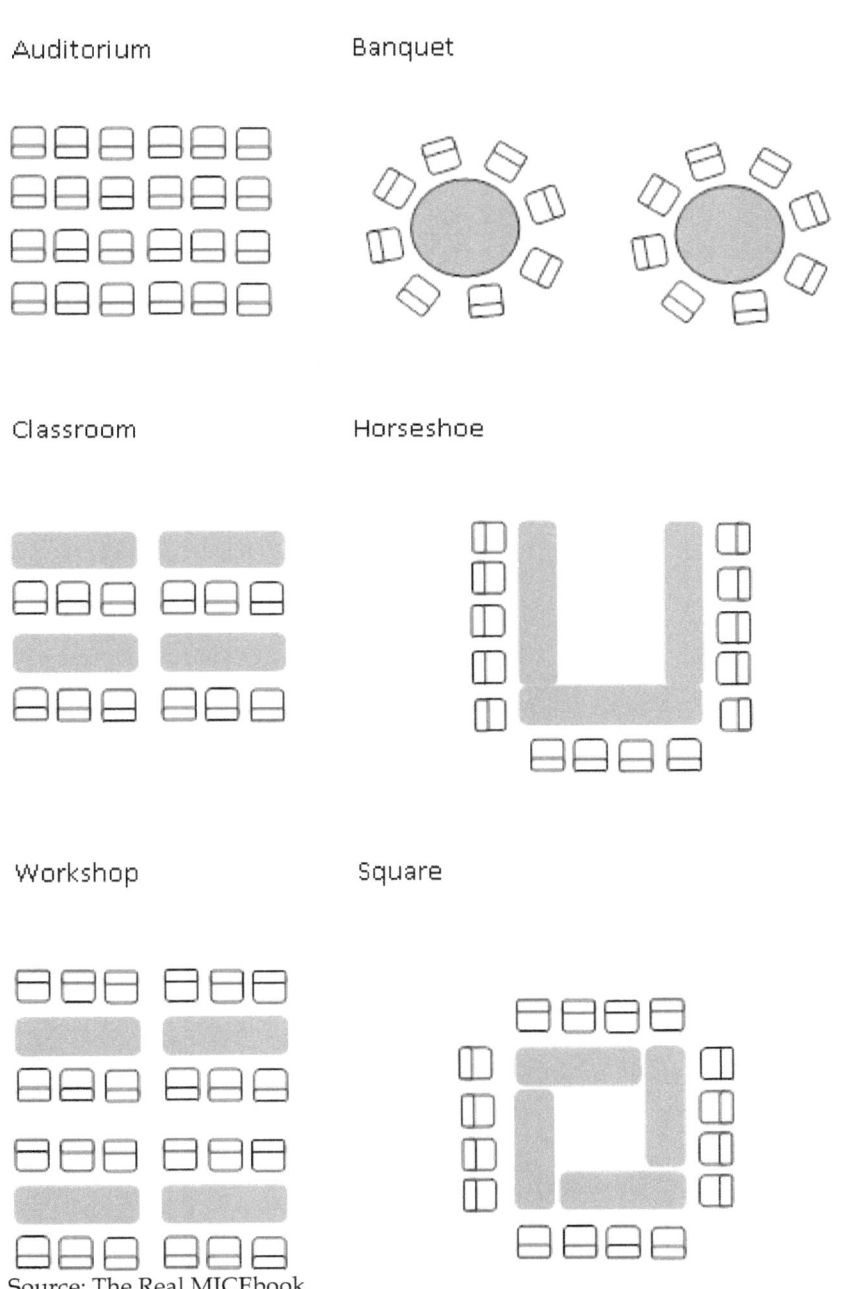

Auditorium

Banquet

Classroom

Horseshoe

Workshop

Square

Source: The Real MICEbook